The Wild West in American History

RAILROADERS

Written by Leonard J. Matthews
Illustrated by Geoffrey Campion and others

Library of Congress Cataloging-in-Publication Data

Matthews, Leonard, 1920-
  Railroaders / by Leonard Matthews.

   p. cm. — (The Wild West in American history)
  Summary: Traces the history of American railroading, focusing on the building of the transcontinental railroad and the daily life and hardships of the construction workers.
  ISBN 0-86625-366-1
  1. Railroads — West (U.S.) — History — 19th century — Juvenile literature. 2. Railroad construction workers — West (U.S.) — History — 19th century — Juvenile literature. [1. Railroads — West (U.S.) —History. 2. West (U.S.) — History.] I. Title. II. Series.
HE27631988a   88-12104
385'.0978 - dc19   CIP
                                                         AC

Rourke Publications, Inc.
Vero Beach, Florida 32964

RAILROADERS

RAILROADERS

Although it may seem surprising to us now, railways were in use four hundred years ago in the European country of Transylvania.

They were wooden tramways. Two hundred years later, similar wooden railways were still being used in England to transport coal from the mines to loading depots along riversides. The coal trucks were pulled by men or horses, because no form of steam, gas, or electrical power was available

By 1804, the wooden rails had been replaced by metal ones, but the trucks were still being hauled by men and horses. Then an Englishman named Richard Trevithick proudly exhibited his invention, a double-acting high-pressure steam engine and a steam road locomotive.

Unfortunately, because cast-iron is a brittle metal, the first locomotives were so heavy that they broke down often and Trevithick was laughed at and mocked by many people.

Then along came two Englishmen, George Stephenson and his son, Robert. They were determined to overcome all resistance to the use of steam locomotives as a new form of transport.

They constructed the first locomotive with a multi-tubular boiler and named it *Rocket*. In 1829, at Rainhill in England, the *Rocket* reached a maximum speed of 29 miles per hour. Railroads as we know them today had come to stay. Today's locomotives travel much faster, usually around 100 miles per hour.

THE IRON HORSE

*A*t the time George and Robert Stephenson invented their *Rocket*, people in the eastern part of America were planning railroads. But at that time their plans did not include the use of steam power. They expected the cars to be pulled by horses along wooden tracks.

When it became known that steam-powered locomotives had been invented in England, a Horatio Allen, a young engineer who worked for the Delaware and Hudson Canal Company, went to England to see these wonder engines. They were called Iron Horses. He was so impressed that he ordered four of them. On May 13, 1829, the first English locomotive arrived in New York City.

Some people thought it looked like a huge grasshopper. On the front was the face of a big, fierce-looking lion. The engine's name was *The Stourbridge Lion* because it had been built by a company in Stourbridge, England.

Horatio Allen brought his *Lion* to life with steam, and thousands of people flocked to see the curious locomotive. But there were no tracks on which to run it, so Allen shipped it by river and canal to Honesdale, Pennsylvania. There he gave it a trial run on a flimsy wooden track. The run was successful, and Horatio Allen became the first man to make a trip on a steam engine operated on the tracks of an American railroad.

The Iron Horse had come to stay. From then on the design of steam engines rapidly improved and steel rails replaced wooden tracks.

Horatio Allen later became the chief engineer of the South Carolina Railroad Company. He designed a new American locomotive in Charleston, South Carolina. Named *Best Friend of Charleston*, it had a vertical boiler shaped like a wine bottle. It was America's first regular passenger train and it operated over what was then the longest railroad in the world – 136 miles.

Unfortunately, the fireman operating it one June day in 1831 knew nothing about the power of steam. He became annoyed by the hissing of the safety valve, and he tied down the lever. The pressure of steam built up, and the *Best Friend of Charleston* exploded, killing

The Stourbridge Lion was the first locomotive to be seen in New York. The year was 1829.

the fireman and badly scalding the engineer.

Allen also designed the first "headlight." It was a flat car placed in front of the engine, containing a wood fire burning in sand.

The early American trains were called puffers because of the sound they made. Traveling by rail in those days was not only uncomfortable but dangerous for people riding in open flat cars. Blazing sparks from the smoke stacks showered down on them and set fire to their clothing. Some people put up umbrellas to fend off the flying embers but soon found out this was not a good idea, since the umbrellas caught fire. They were enveloped in clouds of black smoke. When the engine lurched forward or braked with a jerk, passengers were flung out of their seats, which in those days were wooden benches. They landed either on the floor or on top of each other. The trains also tended to jump the track when rounding a curve.

In spite of all the discomfort and danger, traveling by train was something new and exciting. People eagerly crowded into the carriages and onto the open cars to experience the thrill of riding on a train pulled by an Iron Horse.

A Pony Express rider races toward a relay station.

EARLY TRANSPORT

The railroads finally won the West, but other forms of transportation also have their pride of place in American history. In April 1860, the famous Pony Express was the means of transporting mail quickly from St. Joseph, Missouri, to San Francisco, a distance of some 2,000 miles. It took 10 days. Mail was carried by 120 courageous young riders who faced danger from war parties, bandits, blizzards, and raging rivers.

Rider galloped up to relay stations along the route, threw their mail pouches onto a waiting horse, and raced off again, all within two minutes. After riding a certain distance a rider handed his mail over to the next rider waiting at another station.

The Pony Express only lasted a year, because a transcontinental telegraph put them out of service. The founders, Russell, Majors, and Waddell, were heavily in debt. The fees charged for carrying 35,000 items of mail did not cover the cost of running the service.

American industry was growing fast, and the field of transportation was in the lead. A railroad was soon to follow the route of the Pony riders across the Plains and mountains.

The era of the river steamboat started in 1811 and lasted for 60 years. Steamboats were fast, flat-bottomed boats with three or four tiers of decks. They offered passengers every luxury available at the time. Proudly they chugged up and down the Mississippi, Missouri, and other western rivers, smoke billowing from their long funnels. By 1846 there were almost 2,000 steamboats on western rivers, and they were carrying $400 million worth of freight.

Twenty years before a railroad ever spanned the continent, freight wagons pulled by teams of oxen transported goods from Missouri to California in four months. Stagecoaches also carried passengers and mail across the West.

John Butterfield started the famous Overland Mail. His Concord stagecoaches took 24 days to complete the journey from St. Louis. They traveled through desert and mountainous country, and through the home of half a million Indians who were not always friendly.

Russell, Majors, and Waddell also ran a stage line and freight wagons, but the greatest of all freight companies was The American Express Company. It shipped all kinds of goods worth millions of dollars across the West. It invented the C.O.D. (cash on delivery) system, which is still used today. From stagecoaches, the company moved into railroads and then banking. The famous Wells Fargo joined forces with The American Express Company in 1852, and today it is still a part of American Express. Instead of Concord coaches pulled by a team of six horses, though, Wells Fargo uses heavily armored trucks painted the traditional Wells Fargo red.

Pony Express riders, steamboats, freight wagons, and stagecoaches all pointed the way for the great railroads across the West.

THE WAY TO THE WEST

December 9, 1852, was the first time that anyone had ridden on a train west of the Mississippi River. Although the locomotive was owned by the Pacific Railroad of Missouri and was named *The Pacific*, it did not go anywhere near the West Coast. The entire distance it chugged its way along was a five-mile stretch of track running westward from St. Louis, Missouri. But it was the start of the rails going westward.

For many years people had been talking about a transcontinental railroad. At the time it seemed like an impossible dream, just as putting men on the moon once seemed impossible. The railroad dream became a reality in 1869, and 100 years later, in 1969, man set foot on the moon.

Building a railroad spanning 2,000 miles from Missouri to California was the greatest engineering feat in American history.

The first big problem was to find a suitable route across America. It would have to cross the vast plains, inhabited by thousands of Indians and millions of buffalo. It would have to climb up and over high mountain ranges and cross burning deserts.

The Civil War had started in 1861, and the North and South were split over the slavery issue and states' rights. Each side had its own idea as to where a railroad should be built.

Army engineers and politicians suggested different routes, some favoring the trails blazed by the early explorers, fur trappers, and Indian traders. The Indian trails across the West discovered by frontiersmen were not always suitable for the laying of railroad tracks.

Two brilliant surveyors, Theodore Judah and Major General Grenville Dodge, finally mapped out an acceptable route for the transcontinental railroad. The route they chose followed the basic path of the Emigrant Trail, along which pioneers and miners had traveled to reach California. It was not an easy route, as it meant going over the Sierra Nevada and Rocky Mountains, blasting through rock and granite to make tunnels and tracks on which to lay the rails.

The path they chose for the railroad would join the Pacific coast to more than 30,000 miles of track existing at that time in the Eastern states.

Theodore Judah surveyed the route east from Sacramento, California. Grenville Dodge surveyed it from Omaha, Nebraska, westward. The Pacific Railroad Act was drawn up largely through Judah's efforts, and President Lincoln signed it in July of 1862. The transcontinental railroad would be built by two companies, the Central Pacific and Union Pacific.

The Central Pacific broke ground at Sacramento in January 1863 and the Union Pacific at Omaha in the December of that year.

General Grenville M. Dodge was the chief engineer for the Union Pacific, the railroad which was built from Omaha in the east to the Far West. Starting in 1865, it was completed in 1869 after four years of constant dangers and hardship.

But before the actual construction could start, a lot of money was needed and land had to be obtained. By July 1865, however, when the Civil War had ended, there was sufficient money and land for the mammoth project to go ahead.

Much of the land over which the railroad would run was stolen from the Indians. It was the grazing ground of their buffalo. Whenever they got the chance, the enraged warriors would gallop alongside a train and shoot at the hated Iron Horse.

The construction gangs of the Union Pacific were made up of a mixed bunch of tough men. There were many Irish and some British and Germans. There were Civil War veterans from both the North and South and freed slaves.

Workers had to be tough to lay miles of track. The railroad took four years to build, and there was fierce competition between the crews of both railroads as to who laid the most track at one time. In April 1869, just before the two railroads joined, both the Central and the Union Pacific claimed the laying of 10 miles of track in one day, a mighty feat indeed.

THE ATTACK AT PLUM CREEK

*I*t did not take the Indians long to realize that the Iron Horse was their greatest enemy.

Gangs of railroad workers poured into western Nebraska and southeastern Wyoming in the hundreds. They invaded the hunting grounds of the Sioux and Cheyennes as they laid the tracks of the Union Pacific. The furious Indians sounded their war drums, donned their war paint, and attacked the invaders.

They took their revenge out on the telegraph wires, tearing them down. They believed the humming of the wires was bad medicine and would harm them. They ripped up the iron rails. They attacked trains and killed passengers. They took whatever goods the train was carrying.

One famous incident took place at Plum Creek, Nebraska, on August 6, 1867.

A war party of Cheyennes led by their chief, Turkey Leg, was riding along an ancient Indian trail when they came across the tracks of the Union Pacific. Lying alongside the rails was a pile of ties, or sleepers. That was just what the warriors needed to cause a wreck.

Their hearts were filled with anger because they were escaping from an army patrol that was scouring the territory for warring Indians. Here was the chance they had been waiting for. They made a barricade of the ties and laid them across the track. Ripping the wires from a nearby telegraph pole, they lashed the ties to the rails.

They had no idea when a train would be coming along, but they were prepared to wait hours if necessary. So they took cover in some bushes close by and waited.

Some miles away at Plum Creek Station, the telegraph repairman, who was a young Englishman by the name of William Thompson, noticed that the line had gone dead. It was his job to see that the telegraph was working at all times on his section of the railroad. He sprang into action, for he had to find the break in the line and repair it as quickly as possible.

He and five section hands jumped on a hand-pump car loaded with a spool of new wire, repair tools and six Spencer rifles, and set off down the track.

It was dark by then and they were going at speed, so they never saw the barricade. The hand-pump car smashed into it, and all six men went flying through the air, landing heavily on the ground.

The next instant the Cheyennes, uttering harsh war cries, rushed from their hiding place with rifles blazing. The five section hands were killed outright. Thompson staggered to his feet, groping for one of the Spencers that had been flung out of the car. Before he could reach it he was shot in the arm by a Cheyenne and knocked to the ground.

Unfortunately for the young man, he had long blonde hair, and this was something no warrior could resist. The next minute Thompson's scalp was being lifted.

He lay still and pretended to be dead. Through pain-filled eyes he watched the war party picking up the tools and waited for a chance to crawl away.

With the tools and the spool of wire from the pump car, the Indians improved their ambush. They unbolted two rails, wrenched them up, and with much grunting and heaving managed to bend them in two. They lashed them up with wire and then laid them across the track.

While they were doing this, Thompson crawled silently away.

The night freight train was pounding up from the east and the waiting Cheyennes saw its faint oil-fired head lamp in the distance. They brandished their rifles over their heads.

Like Thompson, the engine driver failed to see the barricade until it was too late. The engine crashed into it, killing him and the fireman.

At the end of the train the construction crew leapt out of the carriage and hearing Indian war cries, they tore away in the darkness and made their escape back to Plum Creek. On the way they managed to flag down a following freight train just in time to avoid a second collision.

Meanwhile, at the wreck, the Indians set about looting the train and to their joy found a barrel of whiskey. They carried off their loot and disappeared into the night, triumphant at their victory over the hated enemy.

The hand-pump car smashed into the barricade as a yelling mob of Cheyennes sped forward. They intended to kill all the railroad men without mercy. Only one man was to survive.

Somehow William Thompson found the strength to crawl for miles before he was rescued and taken to a doctor. He survived his terrible ordeal and later returned to his job.

The Union Pacific construction crews faced danger from the hostile Indians, but their rivals, the Central Pacific, faced a different kind of danger. For them, danger came in the form of accidents and severe weather conditions when laying tracks over the formidable Sierra Mountains and across the parched deserts.

The Indians were fighting for their lives, their land, and their buffalo. They had seen their great herds slaughtered by thousands by buffalo hunters. Now the Iron Horse had

The tracklayers were drilled relentlessly until they could spike down track so speedily that finally they reached the amazing rate of ten miles per day. The workers were often bribed to work faster with extra tobacco and double wages.

invaded their land, bringing another danger to their buffalo. A new sport had sprung up among the white men. As the great shaggy beasts quietly grazed alongside the railroad tracks, passengers shot them with rifles from the moving trains.

In frustration, the Indians kept up their attacks on the construction crews and the situation got so bad the U.S. Indian-Fighting Army was called in to protect the railroad workers. By 1868, nearly 5,000 soldiers were patrolling along and around the tracks. In despair, the Sioux and Cheyenne, two mighty Plains tribes, knew their days were numbered. Eventually they would all be rounded up and placed on reservations. Their freedom, their land, and their buffalo would be taken away from them forever.

To protect the construction crews as they worked on the railroads, the U.S. Indian-Fighting Army was sent in and one of the commanding officers was none other than that well-known cavalier of the Plains, Lt. Col. George A. Custer.

TRACKS ACROSS THE WEST

General Grenville Dodge, was chief engineer of the Union Pacific. John (Jack) Casement, another Civil War general, was the track-laying boss. Although Jack was only five feet, four inches tall, he was a tough commander and quickly earned the respect of the big, burly men in the track-laying gangs. His brother, Dan, assisted him and was even shorter. Like Jack, though, no one ever tangled with him.

Jack Casement signed a contract with Thomas C. Durant, who was vice-president and general manager of the Union Pacific, to lay track for $750 a mile. He drilled his men relentlessly until they could spike down track speedily and with precision. In fact, no one had ever used such an efficient rail-laying routine before.

Men worked ahead of the train, grading and leveling the road-bed and dropping the ties into place, five for each section of track.

Lightweight carts loaded with 16 rails, spikes, bolts, and rail couplings (called fish-plates), were each hauled by a galloping horse to the newest sections of track. Men working in pairs lifted each rail, which weighed between 500 to 700 pounds, out of the cart, ran forward, and as the foreman yelled "Down!" they dropped the rail onto the ties. Men with a notched wooden gauge spaced each pair of rails at four feet, eight and one half inches apart. Then clampers fixed the rails in place and the spike men swung their mauls (long-handled hammers) and knocked in the spikes.

At first the crews laid a mile of track a day, but when the rival crews of the Union Pacific and Central Pacific got closer to each other the pace quickened to two, three, and even more miles a day. Jack Casement was known to offer bribes to his men ranging from extra tobacco to double pay if they would work faster.

The work train was the nerve center of the track-laying operation. It moved along the freshly laid track carrying the necessary supplies for the laying of track ahead of it. It was pushed by an engine, instead of being pulled. In front were flat cars carrying all the tools and a blacksmith shop. Then came the bunkhouse-on-wheels, three huge boxcars, 85 feet long with three tiers of bunks where some 300 to 400 men slept. After that came the dining car, a car divided into a kitchen, washroom and storeroom, a car for the carpenter's shop, and a car for the engineer's office and the telegrapher and his equipment. It was like a miniature town on wheels.

The railroad worker's life was not an easy one. The pay was only a few dollars a day. The food was a steady diet of beef, beans, pie, bread, and coffee. The work was back-breaking and the men toiled in freezing cold and burning heat. There was always the threat of accidents and the fear of Indian attacks.

On one occasion Grenville Dodge was having a meeting with several government officials in his private car on a train at the end of a track. They were at a camp 100 miles west of Overton, Nebraska. A war party of Sioux suddenly swooped down on the camp. Workmen, used to such attacks, dropped their tools and grabbed their rifles, which were always close at hand, and blazed away at the warriors.

General Dodge ran out of his car, firing his revolver and encouraging his men. The Indians soon retreated to a nearby ravine, and Dodge was all for going after them but the men refused. They told him they had to defend themselves against attack, but they were paid to build a railroad, not to fight Indians.

These mobile towns were made up of gamblers, saloonkeepers, thieves, and dance hall girls. They were all out to make a "fast buck" by taking from the rail workers their hard-earned wages.

The track layers had nothing to amuse or entertain them at the end of a tough day's work. When the camp followers came along, the men could not get to the tents fast enough on payday to drink and gamble their wages away. Some of the dance hall girls carried little derringer pistols and held up the workers before they even reached the tents.

Fights broke out among the railmen, gamblers, and saloonkeepers. Many of them were severely hurt, and some were even killed.

Grenville Dodge, who ran his construction crews like a military operation, did not interfere with his men losing their money. What

With little to amuse them at the end of a day's work, the reckless railroad crews drank and gambled away their hard-earned wages.

they did with their pay was their own business. But when it came to his men being wounded or killed, he put his foot down. It was difficult enough to get hard-working crews, and he was not going to lose men at the makeshift towns that sprang up around his Union Pacific. He asked Jack Casement to do something about it.

Casement chose a few of his rough, burly, muscled men, and they started visiting the gambling tents and saloons. After a few fights and shootings, the people who operated the lawless towns got the message. The railmen still visited the tents and lost their money gambling or spent it on alcohol, but apart from a few brawls, the killing and serious wounding stopped. Casement continued his clean-up routine wherever the tent towns sprang up.

The weather was another hazard the railmen had to face. Summer storms could become violent with torrential rains, roaring thunder, and vivid lightning. Then came the snow of winter. The winter of 1867–68 was the worst on record. Winds called "blue northers" blew in from Canada, bringing tons of snow and halting the work of the Union Pacific altogether.

In January the Missouri River was frozen 16 inches thick at Omaha, strong enough to take the weight of an engine. Jack Casement decided to make good use of the frozen river.

Large supplies of materials he needed were stored on the opposite bank of the Missouri. Rather than waste time waiting for the ice to thaw so the materials could be ferried across the river, he laid temporary rails on the ice and was able to bring the supplies across easily and quickly.

After that came the spring thaw, which sent the melting snow rushing down the mountains and flooding the plains. The damage was heartbreaking to the railroad workers who saw miles of track, bridges, telegraph lines, and embankments all washed away. Work had to begin all over again.

Thomas C. Durant was in charge of the financing of the Union Pacific and was known to keep a good share of the money for himself. He wanted to extend the route mapped out by General Dodge in order to get more money from the government. When Dodge heard about it, he was able to prevent Durant's proposed scheme. Construction went ahead as planned.

The transportation of building materials for the railroad to the railhead was made much easier when the Chicago and Northwestern Railroad brought its tracks to the Missouri

River. Materials were ferried across the river to Omaha and were then loaded onto cars and taken down the track to where they were needed.

Getting sufficient wood for the ties was also made easier as the Union Pacific moved westward. Before reaching Wyoming, Jack Casement sent 1800 woodchoppers and haulers to the forests of Wyoming. By the time the rails reached the boundary of that vast territory, 100,000 ties were ready and waiting.

As the laying of track extended westward from Omaha, so people intent on making money began flocking to where construction crews had their camps. Tent towns sprang up and moved across the West, following the railroad workers.

Some of the mobile camp towns remained where they were as settlers in the thousands arrived on trains from the East and needed somewhere to live. Towns such as North Platte, Julesburg, Cheyenne, and Laramie became permanent settlements.

By present-day standards, these frontier towns were rough and wild at first. Soon, though, lawmen moved in and kept peace with their six-guns.

Herds of buffalo would often charge across the tracks, bringing the trains to a jolting halt.

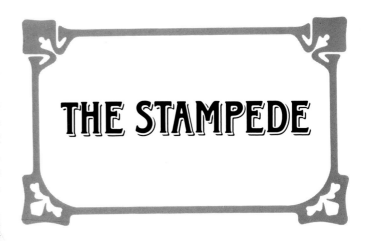

THE STAMPEDE

Stampeding buffalo followed a leader. Wherever it ran, they were close behind, shaking the ground with the pounding of their hooves. If a train frightened them, they would often race alongside it, overtake it, and run across the track right in its path, bringing the train to a halt. These instances gave any passengers with rifles the chance to get in some shooting. With so many animals at close range, they could kill a great number in a short time.

After several trains had been held up by buffalo crossing the tracks, a water-spouting device was fitted to the engine in an attempt to chase the animals off. The jet of water was strong enough to stop a beast in its tracks, which would cause confusion in the herd.

They often turned to milling around in circles on either side of the track, with the moving train between them.

On one occasion Thomas Durant took a party of celebrities by train to see construction crews at work on the line a couple of hundred miles west of Omaha. After watching the sweating workers laying the rails and banging in the spikes, they all retired to the train for a meal of roast duck and champagne. Afterwards, Durant staged a buffalo hunt for the benefit of his guests. It was probably a shoot from the train windows, because if there were any buffalo grazing nearby the guests could easily have scared them into stampeding alongside the train.

There was a manpower shortage in California so the Central Pacific Railroad hired Chinese workers. To everyone's astonishment, the Chinese proved to be brave and reliable. As time went on, thousands of these tough Orientals were hired.

THE CENTRAL PACIFIC

*C*harles Crocker was the general superintendent of the Central Pacific Railroad. He was a big, tough man, always out on site directing construction and frequently grabbing a shovel or a pick when an extra hand was needed. It was his job to build the railroad eastward from California across the Sierra Nevada Mountains to link up with the Union Pacific, which was heading across endless plains toward the Rocky Mountains.

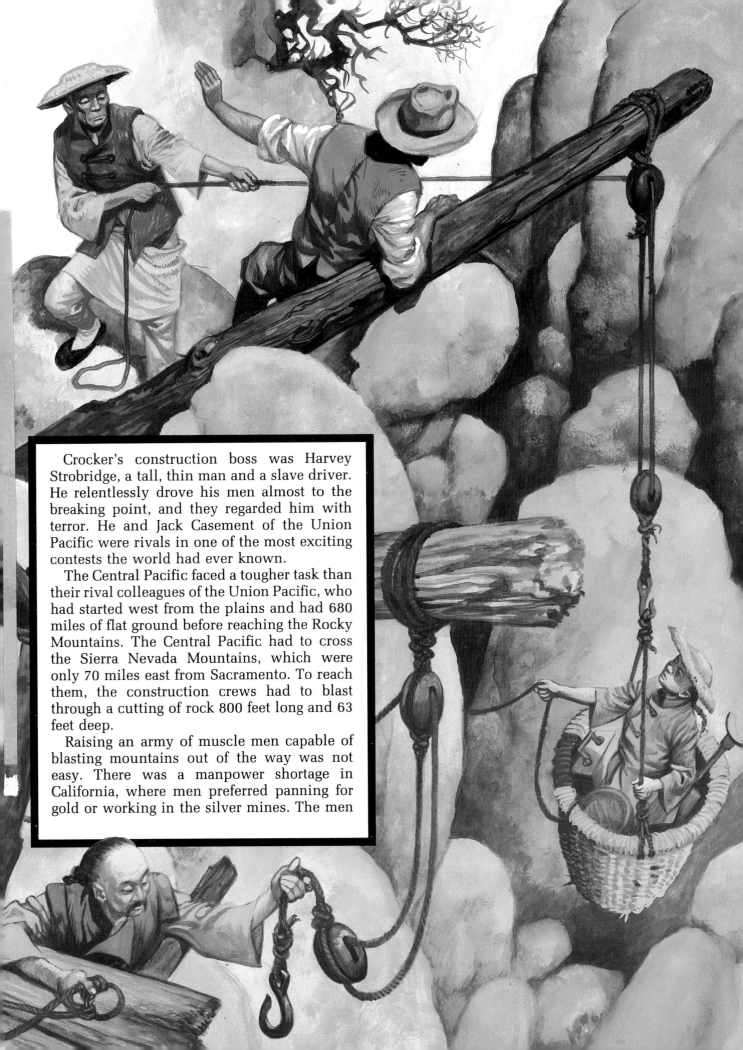

Crocker's construction boss was Harvey Strobridge, a tall, thin man and a slave driver. He relentlessly drove his men almost to the breaking point, and they regarded him with terror. He and Jack Casement of the Union Pacific were rivals in one of the most exciting contests the world had ever known.

The Central Pacific faced a tougher task than their rival colleagues of the Union Pacific, who had started west from the plains and had 680 miles of flat ground before reaching the Rocky Mountains. The Central Pacific had to cross the Sierra Nevada Mountains, which were only 70 miles east from Sacramento. To reach them, the construction crews had to blast through a cutting of rock 800 feet long and 63 feet deep.

Raising an army of muscle men capable of blasting mountains out of the way was not easy. There was a manpower shortage in California, where men preferred panning for gold or working in the silver mines. The men

Crocker did sign on were mostly Irish immigrants. And then he got an idea that saved the situation: he would hire Chinese workers.

Many Chinese had come to California in search of gold. When the gold rush years ended, hundreds of them stayed on, working as house servants and in restaurants, or as laborers. They were hated and persecuted by the white people because they worked for less money and worked harder. People made fun of their blue cotton trousers, their conical straw hats, and their pigtails.

When Crocker ordered Strobridge to hire 50 Chinese on a trial basis, the construction boss nearly exploded. He was not going to have little Orientals work for him. They ate bamboo shoots and rice and drank tea and looked so frail a puff of wind would blow them over. But Crocker was his boss, so he had to obey orders.

To everyone's astonishment the little Chinese, who averaged under five feet tall, proved brave, tough, reliable workers, willing to tackle any job no matter how hard. In time even Strobridge came to respect them, and Crocker hired thousands of Chinese, even bringing them directly from China.

Fifty-seven miles out from Sacramento the Chinese, who were known as "Crocker's Pets," proved they were as courageous as they were reliable. The surveyors had decided that the rails would have to go along a ledge cut around a huge rocky overlay jutting out from the side of a mountain, 1,400 feet above a river.

Strobridge knew his Chinese crew never refused to do a job, so he set them to do an extremely dangerous task. They wove baskets of reeds large enough to hold a man armed with an iron hand drill, a sledge, and a keg of black powder. The workers were lowered down the cliff face in the baskets. Swaying perilously against the side of the mountain, they drilled and pounded two-and-a-half-inch-wide holes in the rock. They filled the holes with powder and set fuses in them. They were then hauled up to safety just before the explosions rocked the gorge.

The Chinese loved firecrackers because they believed the noise frightened away devils, and they actually enjoyed the deafening ex-

During the snow-swept winter of 1876-1877, many Chinese tracklayers were killed by avalanches. Doggedly, the survivors worked on, determined that nothing would stand in their way. The Central Pacific *would* go through.

plosions in spite of the dangers involved.

Slowly and steadily they blasted through the solid rock and made the required ledge without losing a single man.

After their bravery in blasting a ledge around the rocky outlay, "Crocker's Pets" earned the respect of all the white railroad men. They were amazed at the stamina of the frail-looking little Chinese and were amused that they bathed every day and drank quantities of hot tea. It was tea made with boiling water that helped to prevent the Chinese from getting sick. The white workers drank ditch water and frequently suffered from stomach upsets.

Crocker had faith in them right from the start. He had reasoned that if the Chinese could build the largest piece of masonry in the world, the Great Wall of China, then they could build a railroad. And he was right. Eight thousand workers were put to work on the Summit Tunnel high in the Sierra Nevada Mountains, and 6,000 of them were Chinese. Nine tunnels had to be hollowed out of granite and rock in order for the track to be laid up and through the mountains and down the long steep eastern slope of the mountain range.

The winter of 1866-67 was a terrible one in the Sierras. There were 44 blizzards, one lasting 13 days with no letup. Snow piled up 10 feet high and, blown by strong winds, formed an overhanging mass at the edge of the mountain. The weight of the hardened snow caused it to move, and a great avalanche swept men, equipment, and the workers' pitiful dwellings down into the canyon below. Many Chinese, powerless to save themselves, were killed as they went hurtling down the mountain, caught up in the violent force of the rushing snow.

The Chinese working in the tunnels tackled the granite by standing shoulder to shoulder and chipping away with their picks, a few inches a day. During that time nitroglycerin, a liquid explosive, was discovered. It was more powerful than black powder, and the task of blasting and moving tons of rock was sped up. But there were many accidents.

Strobridge lost his right eye by impatiently going to see why an explosion had not occurred. It went off, and he was caught in the blast. He had to wear a patch over his eye and the Chinese called him "One Eye Bossy Man."

Once a way was cleared through and over the Sierras, gangs of 500 workers followed, hauling huge log sleds that carried three locomotives,

40 cars, and enough rails to cover the mountain route.

Up ahead, the graders were hacking out cuttings and building high timber trestle embankments to prevent the trains from having to climb or descend too sharply. Gangs of Chinese hauled away rock and earth in wheelbarrows and dump carts.

By the spring of 1868 the Central Pacific was through the mountains and the crews had to face the heat of the Nevada desert. Laying track on the flat was far easier than up in the Sierras, though.

The lines of the Central Pacific and Union Pacific were getting closer, but in the early months of 1869 no meeting place had been decided. But the race was on in earnest.

The Union Pacific had to cross the Rocky Mountains, but only had to dig four tunnels. The Central Pacific had to dig 15 tunnels in all. The Echo Summit in the Wasatch Range in Utah was the most difficult to tackle. In their haste to beat their rivals, the Union Pacific construction crews built a temporary looping bypass around the summit instead of tunneling through it. They planned to build the tunnel later.

The converging construction gangs met in the American desert. They were only 50 miles apart, but still no effort was made by the leaders to choose a place for the link-up. The Central Pacific was headed in the direction of Ogden, but the Union Pacific did not seem to know where it was going. Their survey lines overlapped for some miles, and when the grading gangs met and went on to pass each other, they were so close they had to dodge the earth thrown up by the other's blasting charges.

When President Grant heard of this ridiculous situation, he summoned Grenville Dodge to Washington and told him to arrange a meeting with the representatives of both companies and decide where their tracks were to link up.

A meeting was held, and Promontory Point, Utah, was decided upon. It was 56 miles west of Ogden, a waterless basin of sagebrush with mountains on three sides. The date was set for May 8, 1869.

The tracks of the Central Pacific reached Promontory Point on April 30. Charles Crocker and his long-suffering Californians had won the race. They were waiting to jeer and boo the Union Pacific crews when they came into view a week later.

A RAILROAD SPANS THE CONTINENT

The great day dawned. It was May 10, not May 8 as originally planned. Torrential rain for two days and the late arrival of T.C. Durant caused the delay.

Facing each other on the track were the Central Pacific's engine *Jupiter*, with a flared funnel stack, and the Union Pacific's engine *No. 119*, with a straight cylindrical stack.

People were everywhere. The air was filled with excitement. Promontory Point was difficult to reach because it was in such a remote place, but there were probably six or seven hundred people attending the ceremony.

Leland Stanford, governor of California, was involved in a freak accident on the way to Promontory Point. A Chinese timber gang was felling trees in the mountains above the railroad track, and a log rolled down the slope on to the rails along which Stanford's train was traveling from California. The engineer braked hard, but could not avoid hitting the log. The cowcatcher was ripped off, but fortunately no one was hurt. The train crawled slowly to the next depot, and another engine was hitched to the carriages. Stanford arrived safely, bringing with him a silver-headed sledgehammer, a polished laurel tie, and four ceremonial spikes: two gold, one silver, and one combination iron, silver and gold.

Another incident involved Thomas C. Durant. As his Union Pacific train pulled into Piedmont, Wyoming, an armed mob of his own tie cutters surrounded his private car and chained the wheels to the rails. The men informed Durant and his startled associates that they had not received any pay since January and intended holding him prisoner until they received their overdue wages. Durant had no choice but to send a telegram to his New York headquarters requesting the payroll fund be telegraphed to him immediately. This was

Success at last! The tracks of the Union Pacific and the Central Pacific Railroads met at Promontory Point on May 10, 1869. When news of the event was flashed across the continent, the whole of the United States celebrated.

done, and Durant and his guests were free to continue their journey. Because Durant was delayed for two days, the ceremony was held over until May 10.

A company of soldiers of the Twenty-first Infantry formed a double line facing the tracks. Officials from both railroads with their families, friends, photographers, reporters, and construction crews all waited for the ceremony to begin at noon. All of the country eagerly awaited the telegraph message that would signal the joining of the continent by iron rails. An iron spike partially driven into a tie was wired up to the national telegraph system. When struck by a hammer the sound would go out over the wires and the whole country would hear it.

The last pair of rails had been laid and the polished laurel tie was slipped beneath the last joint. The four ceremonial spikes were dropped into place, but it was the iron spike that had to be hammered in.

After Stanford and Dodge made their speeches, Stanford, the highest-ranking official present, raised high the heavy silver-headed sledgehammer. A hush fell over the crowd. He brought it smartly down and missed the spike! Durant then took the sledgehammer, swung it, and also missed. So it was the telegraph operator who sent the signal to the waiting country.

The ceremonial spikes and the laurel tie were removed. Cheering workmen clambered up on both engines. Champagne flowed. Everyone milled round excitedly. Reporters were interviewing the officials, the construction bosses, and the workmen. Photographers took pictures of Grenville Dodge, chief engineer of the Union Pacific, shaking hands with Samuel Montague, chief engineer of the Central Pacific.

Then *Jupiter* backed up and made room for *No. 119* to cross the rail junction on to the Central Pacific's tracks. It gave a blast from its whistle as it moved across on to the tracks of the Union Pacific.

After four years the transcontinental railroad had become a reality, and Iron Horses were ready to race across the American continent.

One of the golden spikes used at the ceremony linking the two railroads was inscribed with the following prayer: "May God continue the unity of our country as this railroad unites the two great oceans of the world."

Leland Stanford, the governor of California, who was so proud of the Central Pacific, had had a train named after him some years before the historical birth of the transcontinental railroad. It was the Central Pacific's first locomotive, the wood-burning *Governor Stanford*. When the tracks were laid from Sacramento to Roseville, a distance of 18½ miles, the *Stanford* made its first trip on April 26, 1864, carrying passengers. The fare for one way was $1.85.

THE OPENING UP OF THE WEST

*M*ay 10, 1869, was one of the greatest days of the century, but it would be some years before the transcontinental railroad was finally finished.

Tunnels had to be completed and flimsy bridges that were erected during the race across the country had to be securely built. Depots were made into proper stations, around which towns soon sprang up. Thousands of settlers, mainly immigrants from Europe, began to use the railroad to take them to new territory where they could start a new life. Building projects started springing up, and trade began to flourish between the east and west coasts.

The railroads altered the lives of the cowboys. When the Kansas Pacific Railroad started transporting cattle back east, their shipping points were small settlements that grew into notorious cowtowns — Abilene, Ellsworth, and Hays City. Thousands of cattle poured into these towns after long drives up from Texas. The tired and thirsty cowboys needed a place to stay before returning to their ranches, so crude hotels, eating houses, and

William F. Cody killed so many buffalos to provide meat for the Kansas Pacific construction crews, he became world-famous as Buffalo Bill.

saloons sprang up like mushrooms. These cattle drives to the railroad towns were responsible for turning the cowboy into a legendary figure. Before that he was just a stock handler on horseback living on a ranch.

At the end of a drive the cowboys were paid off, and in restless, reckless moods, they spent their wages gambling and drinking. They were rough, tough, and wild and would fight at a drop of a hat, using their fists or more often, their guns. Their shoot-outs brought in sheriffs and marshals and the era of the wild and woolly West began. Without the Iron Horse, such changes could not have taken place.

When the tracks of the Kansas Pacific Railroad reached Fort Riley late in the year of **1866, the glory-seeking Lieutenant Colonel George Armstrong Custer had just arrived to** lead the Seventh Cavalry. Their assignment was to keep the Plains Indians away from the railroad.

Working for the Kansas Pacific Railroad was a young man by the name of William F. Cody. He was paid $500 a month to keep the construction crews supplied with buffalo meat. A crack shot with a rifle, he killed so many buffalos that he was nicknamed Buffalo Bill. Without his job with the Kansas Pacific, he might never have become world-famous.

As the building of railroads continued to increase, so fame and fortune was brought to all kinds of people and to all sorts of places. By 1900 there were four more transcontinental railroads across the United States.

THE TRAIN ROBBERS

*I*n the early 1860s, robbing trains was something new to the outlaws who held up stagecoaches and banks.

The first train robbery took place on May 5, 1865, shortly after the end of the Civil War. A band of men, ex-guerrilla fighters of the Civil War, were looking for adventure and easy money. They decided to rob a train owned by

Butch Cassidy, the ruthless bandit who organized the desperate gang known as the Wild Bunch.

the Ohio and Mississippi Railroad. The train was running from St. Louis, Missouri, to Cincinnati, Ohio.

The ruffians derailed the train and as it stopped, they swarmed onto it. Some went through the cars, holding up the passengers at gunpoint and taking all their money and valuables. The rest of the gang robbed the express car of its contents.

Grabbing their loot, they dashed to the river bank where they had moored some skiffs. They managed to escape down the river and were never heard of again. No one ever knew who they were.

The first organized gang of outlaws to stage a train robbery was the Reno Gang. Their first robbery took place near the town of Seymour, Indiana, on October 6, 1866, and was an Adams Express Company train. They got away with $10,000 from the express car.

News of their daring robbery got about and two other outlaws, Walter Hammond and Michael Colleran, decided to follow in the Renos' footsteps. They also robbed an Adams car and got away with $8,000.

The Reno Gang was blamed for the second robbery. They were so angry when they heard about it that they tracked down the offenders and coolly turned them over to the law!

The success of the Reno Gang got the notorious Jesse James and Cole Younger thinking, and they decided to do some train robbing, too. Their first job was a Rock Island and Pacific Railroad train, which they believed was carrying a large shipment of gold from the west coast to Chicago.

On the night of July 21, 1873, they derailed the train a few miles outside the town of Adair, Iowa. But much to their disappointment, the safe in the express car only contained $3,000. After that they pulled off several more successful train robberies, including one near the town of Sedalia, Missouri, when they got away with $14,000. Cole Younger had broken open the safe with a sharp-pointed pick.

It was Butch Cassidy and his Wild Bunch who robbed a Union Pacific train. In the small hours of the morning of June 2, 1899, near Wilcox, Wyoming, the gang flagged down the train. Cassidy and his boys uncoupled the express car and blew it up. Then they dynamited the safe, and the explosion blew thousands of bank notes up in the air. They managed to scoop up $30,000 and made their getaway safely.

The Wild Bunch pulled off three more train robberies and got away with them. When the Pinkerton detectives failed to catch them, the desperate Union Pacific officials offered to pardon Cassidy and give him a job as an express guard.

They promised a good salary, but Butch was not interested. He promptly proceeded to plan another robbery that was also successful. So the Union Pacific decided to form a squad of crack-shot riflemen and put them on a special high-speed train with orders to bring in the Wild Bunch.

But they were too late. Cassidy decided the time had come to leave the country, since things were getting too hot for him. He and the Sundance Kid, Harry Longbaugh, went to South America and carried on with their train robbing activities down there.

Train robbers came up with various ways of stopping trains. They altered the signals, flagged them down, or held them up at water stops. They did not like derailing trains after several accidents had occurred in which people were killed. They did not want to kill anyone, only rob them, and they only shot people who got in their way!

A RAILROAD WAR

For four years a battle raged between the construction crews of the Atchison, Topeka and Sante Fe line and the Denver and Rio Grande railroad. Both were laying tracks south from Colorado into New Mexico in 1876, looking for freight markets.

William Strong was the general manager of the Santa Fe, and William J. Palmer was the founder of the Rio Grande. With both railroads competing with one another, there were bitter fights and a series of lawsuits in the two years it took them to reach Raton Pass, New Mexico.

In 1868, the silver mines at Leadville, Colorado, were producing 100,000 pounds of ore a day. A railroad was desperately needed to transport the silver. The race between the Santa Fe and the Rio Grande to reach Leadville was on.

The only way to reach Leadville was through the Royal Gorge of the Arkansas River. It seemed impossible to build a railroad through it. The cliff walls were 1,000 feet high and they narrowed down to 30 feet in some places, hardly space enough to lay a track. But Strong and Palmer began working their way towards the canyon.

They each got up to some cunning tricks to try to stop the other, including hiring gangs of guerrillas to delay and sabotage each other's work on the tracks. The famous marshal of Dodge City, Bat Masterson, was one of the gunfighters hired by the Santa Fe to protect the crews, while the Rio Grande hired local sheriffs.

Bridges were burned, survey stakes were moved, and road beds were buried under man-made avalanches.

Palmer's graders swam across the Arkansas River and built a crude fort so they could fire on the Santa Fe crews opposite.

Each crew swarmed on the other's trains and captured each other's depots. At one point Palmer's men killed two of Strong's men and wounded two others. Bat Masterson was unable to protect the Santa Fe workmen.

Finally after four years of dirty fighting on both sides, the war came to an end. The men financing the railroads had to stop the costly violence, and in 1880 a compromise was reached.

The Rio Grande got the line to Leadville and agreed to pay the Santa Fe for the track it had

It was the notorious Jesse James gang that derailed a Rock Island and Pacific train on July 21, 1873.

constructed in the gorge. Sante Fe was given the line to El Paso and St. Louis. Later, the Denver and Rio Grande extended to Salt Lake City, where it connected with the Union Pacific. The Atchison, Topeka and Sante Fe eventually extended to California and was to become one of the most profitable railroads in the United States.

But during construction, more violence occurred between these two railroads than between the Union Pacific and Central Pacific during the building of the transcontinental railroad.

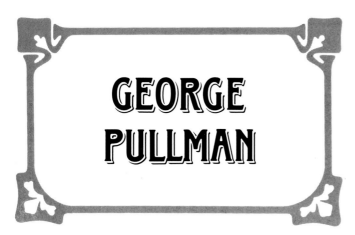

GEORGE PULLMAN

George Pullman never built a railroad, but his name is one of the best known in the history of American railroading.

When people first started traveling by train, the cars were fitted with rows of narrow wooden benches. George Pullman was determined to improve traveling conditions. He wanted passengers to have comfortable seats and berths to sleep in on long journeys.

He managed to persuade the Chicago and Alton railroad to let him have two coaches, and these he turned into crude sleeping cars. All he did was to install hinged upper berths which could be folded up against the car ceiling when not in use, and hinged seats with backs which could be flattened for people to lie back.

The railroad company agreed to try them out on their passengers, and although they were uncomfortable because they were not upholstered, the travelers liked the idea. So Pullman's next step was to upholster the berths, the seats, and the seat backs. From that start, he began designing luxurious sleeping cars with plush seats, fresh linen, and fancy furnishings.

In 1864, he built his own sleeping car, which he named the *Pioneer*. It was roomy and comfortable, but he had made it too wide to go through stations and too high for most bridges. Much to his disappointment no railroad company wanted it. And then, through the tragic assassination of Abraham Lincoln, a use was found for the *Pioneer*.

Because of its roomy interior, it was decided that it would be most suitable to take President Lincoln's coffin to Illinois, where he was to be buried. That meant the stations along the route had to be widened to take the car. This was not such a big problem after all, and so Pullman's car was accepted.

In 1867, he formed the Pullman Palace Car Company, and later he built a huge plant with a town around it, which became known as Pullman, Illinois. Today Pullman is part of Chicago.

In the early days of the railroads there were no dining cars on trains, or any station restaurants west of Topeka. On long journeys trains stopped from time to time to allow cooks to build a fire beside the track and prepare what we call today a barbecue. They cooked buffalo steaks, bacon and other foods. All classes of passengers had their meals out in the open alongside the track.

George Pullman decided something should be done about that, so he built dining cars where passengers could dine in comfort and enjoy delicious meals.

On May 15, 1869, five days after the joining of the rails at Promontory Point, the first transcontinental passenger service was formed. It ran every day. Westbound passengers boarded the Pacific Express at Omaha, bound for Sacramento. Across the continent, eastbound passengers boarded the Atlantic Express at Sacramento, bound for Omaha. It was a 2,000-mile trip and took about four days at a cost of around $100.

Speed and comfort was what travelers wanted, and the wealthy first class passengers got the comfort, thanks to George Pullman's efforts. In addition to his luxurious sleeping and dining cars, there were his magnificent parlor cars. Such luxury is unheard of today in our modern trains.

The poor third-class passengers paid the lowest fare and so had the worst accommodations. They were cowhands, miners, hunters, immigrants, and Indians. But many of them, in later years, made their fortunes out West and no doubt enjoyed the luxuries of first-class travel, thanks to George Pullman.

Bands of outlaw guerrillas were hired by the two railroad companies, the Atchison, Topeka and Santa Fe on one side and the Denver and Rio Grande on the other.

THE RAILROAD HEROES

The real heroes of the railroads were the men who actually built them, the construction crews who with grit and grim determination pitted their lives and skill against high mountains, parched deserts, raging torrents, avalanches, harsh weather conditions, and Indian attacks. It was through their blood, sweat, and unending hard work that the vast United States is now crisscrossed with fine railroads.

Another great transcontinental railway, the Canadian Pacific, spans the east and west coasts of Canada. The intrepid workers who built it suffered the same hardships and shared the same courage as the crews of the American transcontinental railroad.

Built by William Cornelius Van Horne, it was begun in 1881 and finished by 1885. This railroad, too, had to be cut through the Rocky Mountains.

Twelve thousand workers blasted away mountaintops, bored tunnels, drained swamps, and diverted rivers. It was so cold in winter the tracks had to be kept warm to prevent them from cracking. The Canadians were as proud of their transcontinental railroad as the Americans were of theirs, and with just cause. Van Horne loved building railroads. In 1902, he built one in Cuba, and his last project was a railroad in Guatemala in 1908.

One more great railroader must be mentioned. He was James Jerome Hill. Born in 1838, he was a man of lowly beginnings. His business life started in St. Paul, Minnesota, working for various steamship lines. As a young man, still not yet 30 years old, he was selling wood and coal to a Midwestern railroad and at the same time running a small steamship line on the famous Red River, between Minnesota and North Dakota.

He was 40 years old when he and some other rich men, learning that the St. Paul and Pacific railroad was in deep money trouble, took control. Under his clever management, the railroad became a success. From then on, there was no holding back J. J. Hill. He became one of the greatest and most famous railroad empire-builders. He completed the Great Northern railroad in 1893 and shortly afterwards took over the Northern Pacific. He spent the rest of his long life building a railroad empire. When he died in 1916, he left more than $53 million.

Although giant airliners cross the United States and Canada daily and have become the quickest means of travel, they have never totally replaced trains, nor are they likely to.

Trains play a vital part at election time when politicians need them for whistle-stop campaigning. They carry celebrities to outlying areas where normally the residents would be unable to see any famous people in person. They haul heavy freight.

For people who are not in a hurry, travel by rail is leisurely and comfortable. Passengers can view the varied and often breathtaking scenery from the wide windows or from the observation cars.

Trains and aircraft may be in competition, but both are necessary means of transportation. From a train crossing the continent passengers can follow the route taken by courageous pioneers in covered wagons. From an aircraft they can look down with awe and wonder as to how the pioneers ever made their way over such formidable mountain ranges and crossed such wide rivers and empty deserts.

Rail chief Cornelius Van Horne, who was justly proud of achievements not only in Canada but also in Cuba and Guatemala. (Photo: Courtesy Canadian Pacific Archives).

Construction crews not only endured the hardships of the punishing weather but had to be ready at all times for sudden Indian attacks. Many workers died fighting.

IN THE DAYS OF THE RAILROADERS

1700's	A simple wooden rail is used to carry coal from underground to the surface in Britain.
1804	Richard Trevithick, an English engineer, builds the first steam engine.
1825	George Stephenson, another English engineer, opens the first railroad ever to carry passengers.
1825	The Erie Canal opens. It takes eight years and $7,000,000 to cover the 362 miles the canal spans. It is a momentous undertaking and an important link between the east and west coasts.
1830	Stephenson builds the Rocket, the first steam engine.
1835	Over 200 railroad charters exist in eleven states.
1848-1849	The California gold rush points up the need for faster transportation to the west.
1850	Congress allows special grants of land to railroad owners to promote settlement of the western territories.
1858	The Southern Overland Mail route begins.
1860	The Pony Express begins a mail run from Missouri to California.
1861	Invented in 1837 by Samuel Morse, the telegraph now links the country from coast to coast.
1862	The Pacific Railroad Act gives two private companies huge tracts of land and millions of dollars to build a railroad to attract settlers to the western states.
1863	Locomotive engineers organize the first successful railroad union.
1864	Regular railway mail begins service.
1864	The Northern Pacific Railroad is chartered.
1869	The tracks of the Central Pacific and Union Pacific are joined at Promontory, Utah, to form the Transcontinental Railroad.
1874	Jesse James and his gang begin robbing trains.
1880	According to a treaty with China, the United States has the right to regulate Chinese immigration. Chinese are used as laborers by the railroad companies.
1881	People of many occupations band together under one union, the Federation of Organized Trades and Labor Unions.
1882	Labor Day is first celebrated.
1882	Congress passes the Exclusion Act which bars further Chinese immigration.
1895	The Baltimore and Ohio Railroad begins the world's first electric main line service.
1897	Boston begins the first subway.
1900	The Wright Brothers build the first glider.
1934	The Zephyr, the first electric passenger train, begins service.
1964	The Japanese invent passenger trains that can travel at speeds of 130 MPH.